7 Common
Threads for Success

7 Common Threads for Success

All The Things You Should Do Before You Open Your Mouth

Michael J. Nicola

ISBN 978-1-365-79497-1

Table of Contents

<u>Acknowledgements</u>

I would first like to thank Gary Flater for all the encouragement and assistance in writing this book as well as his lovely wife Karen for making me look smart with her editing. I would also like to thank all of those people in my career who have mentored and taught me especially those mentioned in this book. And finally to my family who have put up with me being in this business and spending so much time on the road.

<u>Preface</u>

*"The truly great Wholesaler knows that
his product is himself."*
-Nick Murray

Why would anyone want to be a wholesaler, especially in the financial services world? People look at wholesalers and perceive this occupation as glamorous; traveling, eating and drinking at great restaurants and bars, all the while getting paid well to do so. Those of you, who have wholesaled for any time at all, know that there is very little that is glamorous about this life. The only thing on which a wholesaler can fall back on is that if they are successful, they can make a good living. And at times make a very good living.

So what makes a wholesaler successful? Over the course of many years as a Wholesaler, Divisional and National Sales Manager, I have had the opportunity to work for and with some of the most successful people in this industry; like Doug Wood, Scott Logan, Dan Coates, Jack Perry, Steve Scanlon and Mike Roby. They all have their individual styles but they also share common threads that made them very successful. This book is based on those **common threads**.

7 Common Threads For Success deals with preparing and selling yourself before you even open your mouth. That old saying, "you only have one chance to make a first impression", couldn't be truer for a wholesaler.

Whether you are contemplating a career as a financial services wholesaler or you've wholesaled for awhile, I hope you will find some new "threads" or perhaps be reminded of some forgotten "threads" to help you weave a successful wholesaling career

Thread #1: Your Franchise

"The secret of getting ahead is
getting started."
-Mark Twain

Franchise: "The right or license granted by a company to an individual to market its products or services in a specific territory". –Webster's Dictionary

Modern successful franchises that we know so well like Starbucks, McDonald's and Subway, all have similar business practices; you pay them a franchise fee of approximately $250,000 and they supply you with a business blueprint and the all the necessary materials that you need to start that franchise. Then they tell you exactly what to do to make that franchise successful. For instance, there is a manual that McDonald's gives every employee and it trains them what goes first, the ketchup or the pickles.

Wholesaling, whether it's in the financial services industry or the pharmaceutical industry where you're working out of your car, your territory is your franchise. The good news is you're not making a monetary investment in it per se.

You're being hired by a company to manage a territory and that territory is your franchise. The company supplies you with all the tools that you need: literature, cell phones, computers and training. You've not had to spend a dime on any of those things. You are instantly in business. What you need though and what your company is expecting you to do is to take and develop that business, just like you would take and develop a franchise if you owed a McDonald's, a Subway or a Starbuck's. The bad news is you are not given a proven formula for success.

I've known many wholesalers who have made $500,000 to a million dollars and some who have knocked the ball out of the park and have made well over a million dollars. But the really good, successful wholesalers are in that half million to a million dollars consistently year after year. The fact though is that they've not had to put out that big capital expenditure like you would if it you started a Kentucky Fried Chicken. A wholesaler's only investment is to have a relatively decent car and a couple of business suits in his/her closet. Beyond that, it is just time and sweat equity that they put into this to make a great living. So, wholesaling is truly a franchise and it can be a very, very successful franchise without having to put much in the way of hard capital into it.

But the one thing that most wholesalers in the field, regardless of industry, fail to realize is that even though they don't have a monetary investment in their franchise they still need to run it as if they had invested hard dollars in their own business. In other words, they need to run their business like a business.

You also need to continue to invest in yourself. Not only through knowledge and education which you certainly need to do, but you should also establish your own metrics. How do I run this business? What are my goals? What's going to make my franchise a success, not only for me but a success for the company that has entrusted me with this franchise?

In building and running your franchise, there's no sense in reinventing the wheel. There have been many successful people who have come before me. As I mentioned in the preface, I have had some great mentors like Doug Wood and Jack Perry. Those people have done it! They have a lot of great ideas. It's just a matter of taking those ideas and making them your own, not only on the sales side of your franchise but also on the operating side of your business. People who've been successful can share that with you if you take the time to ask them.

I think a wholesaler's business card should read "his or her name, Inc." This is their business; they are just representing a bigger company. It is very much like the McDonald's franchise owner, it is his or her business but they're representing corporate McDonald's along the way. In wholesaling the brand is you.

In closing, a wholesaler may be selling various products, financial services, pharmaceuticals, etc.....but in reality he/she is a business of one. A wholesaler (like you) is a "franchise of one" who has unlimited upside potential. In order to fulfill this unlimited potential, I strongly advise you to take the forthcoming "common threads" to heart to help you become the best wholesaler you can be.

MIKE NICOLA

Thread #2: Attitude

*"Attitude is a little thing that makes
a big difference"
-Winston Churchill*

Wholesalers are no different than anybody else; they are normal people with normal lives. They have issues in their personal lives or professional lives that they must deal with on a daily basis. Everybody in this world does.

I have found that the most successful people are those who are able to set their personal issues aside during their work day. They are capable of maintaining a positive attitude with clients despite having a bad day. Nobody wants to do business with somebody who is upset or angry.

*Its easy to be pleasant when
Life goes by with a song,
But the man worth while
Is the man who can smile
When everything else goes wrong.
-Anonymous*

People want to do business with people who are happy, friendly and pleasant. Part of that positive attitude is loving what one does. If you don't love what you do, if you don't love going out making that next call, then maybe wholesaling is not the job for you. Wholesalers to a certain extent are a bit masochistic, in that they have to learn to handle rejection well. There are many, many "no's" in sales but when you walk out of that office, you need to pick yourself right back up and be very positive going into the next call. The successful sales people I known, always have a "glass half-full" kind of attitude and that's what sets them apart.

Thinking, knowing and believing that not every "no" is permanent, is a part of that positive attitude adjustment. You may be disappointed walking out of a call where you've just gotten the big "no", but they rarely last forever; there's always hope that you can get back in there and find something else that would fit that client's needs. So, short of just being told "to never come back" that shouldn't affect your attitude. There's always another day to come and see that same person and maybe the first three times it's "no," but the next five times are "yes."

Persistence is definitely a key, but you have to have that correct attitude. If you have the attitude that "I'm going to be happy" and "I'm going to be professional about it," you'll realize that persistence can be a powerful friend of yours, in addition to loving what one does.

The other trait that makes a wholesaler and his/her attitude so important is; not only loving what you do, but it's working hard for the people who hired you. There's an old cowboy saying about "riding for the brand". No matter what you think of your immediate supervisor, or what you think of the company, they are paying you. Since they are allowing you to have this franchise, you should have nothing but positive things to say about them and work hard on their behalf. If you're unhappy with the outfit for which you are working, you should then be looking for a new employer. Find someplace else that might work better for you. It's common, and it's certainly human nature, that there will always be personality rubs and some personalities work better with other personalities. Just because you don't get along with, or you don't agree with the attitude of the company you're working for, doesn't mean you're a bad person. It just means you should be working someplace else, so that you can be as successful as you possibly can be.

Attitude is a two-way street. Like I said at the opening of this chapter, "Everybody on a day-to-day basis has their ups and downs." So you have a great attitude but perhaps your client is having a tough day. You have to be able to recognize that.

You should become a student of body language. Not only your own body language, which really conveys your attitude but your client's body language, too. Their body language can also tell a story about where you should go, how hard you should press in some areas. There's a lot to be said for that but again, it's all about attitude. When you step out of your car and you're standing in the lobby of the office building of your client, you should take a deep breath and check

"Do I have the right attitude to make this call?" If you don't, you need to go get a drink of water and sit down for a minute. You need to go take a deep breath and get your head together and get your attitude in the correct position to make a successful call.

After all, it's your brand. Sure you're selling a particular product, but you are selling yourself first…you are selling your brand.

Believe it or not, clients talk amongst themselves and they're just as quick to talk about somebody who always has a negative attitude as fast as they're willing to talk about somebody who has a positive attitude. Both sides of that coin will get translated as your franchise brand throughout your territory.

People want to do business with people with great attitudes.

Thread #3: Appearance

"To establish yourself in the world a person must do all they can to appear already established"
-Francois de La Rochefoucauld

We've talked about how you are a franchise of one. We have also talked about how important attitude is. Let's now talk about appearance. Remember since you are the product, you're selling yourself. I think a lot of people take appearance for granted and don't realize the impact appearance can make.

People are visual. Our clients are visual. What they see is going to affect them much quicker and much deeper than what they hear. So, when you walk into somebody's office, your appearance immediately sets the tone. People will decide whether they like you or even trust you based on appearance. Many wholesalers truly don't understand the significance of appearance. Great wholesalers, regardless of their business, understand that!

When you walk into a client's office especially for the first time they will determine whether they like you or not by what they see in the first 5 to 8 seconds. The author Malcolm Gladwell in his bestselling book *Blink: The Power of Thinking Without Thinking* writes " There can be as much value in the blink of an eye as in months of rational analysis". Now you can make a less than positive immediate impression and eventually work your way out of it with that client but why penalize yourself before you open your mouth? Why not start on a positive note by having that great appearance?

Appearance is not as simple as it may seem, there are a multitude of aspects that come into play. It's more than wearing a wrinkled suit but it's also your shoes, your accessories, your hair, your physical shape, etc. In this chapter, I like to talk about some of the basics.

Let's start with physical appearance, your bodily appearance. Are you in some sort of shape? Is your hair combed? Whether you're a man or a woman, is it neatly combed? Facial hair; I've not seen very many successful wholesalers in my 30 years of doing this who have had beards, goatees or moustaches. Now I know that currently, everybody seems to be into goatees, the two day shadow look, etc, but again very few are successful. Of course there are exceptions. Dan Coates, who was one of the greatest wholesalers to have walked the face of the Earth, had a great moustache but it was part of his character. So, yes there are exceptions. Psychologically it's a trust issue. Psychologists have discovered that even though facial hair may be well groomed, it still elicits a sense of distrust. Again, I'm not disagreeing with the fact that people can be successful in a lot of businesses with facial hair, I'm just suggesting that why wouldn't you do yourself a favor and up the ante on being successful by getting rid of the facial hair.

Other modern appearance trends are tattoos and piercings. In the last 10 years, tattoos have become very, very popular and so have piercings. I would tell you that if you have a tattoo, don't put it on any part of your body that is visible to your client. You don't know what your client's attitude is towards tattoos or piercings, aside from women having their ears pierced. Gentlemen, if you want to be in the financial services business get rid of all piercings. Typically in a business like this people tend to be a little bit more conservative than not. So again, why start at a disadvantage by assuming your client may like tattoos and piercings or worse yet not caring what they think.

I mentioned a wrinkled suit. Typically in the financial services business, to a certain extent in the pharmaceutical business and some other businesses, men and women wear suits. First of all, there's a huge misconception that you need to go out and buy really expensive suits costing a thousand to $1500. Not true! At Nordstrom's you can buy a $300 suit off the rack. Here's the key: go spend another $100 to have it tailored. Proper fit is much more important than a designer label. Once tailored, you are wearing a $300 suit that looks like a $1300 suit. Also, whenever standing it's important that suit coat fits properly so the middle button (not the top button, not the bottom button) can be comfortably buttoned; as it should. Nothing looks worse than having, and I'll use an old expression, "ten pounds of bricks in a five pound sack". If you've gained weight, go get your clothes fitted accordingly. If you lose weight, the same thing, get your clothes fitted. It's very simple to do.

In the financial services business along with other businesses conservative dress is the expectation. So suits should be navy blue, gray, black, or dark pinstripes, stay away from brown. Brown is a distraction, and again, people in financial services business tend not to take people in brown suits quite as seriously as they do people who are in dark suits.

Let's talk about shirts and blouses. For men, it's very simple; white shirts, light blue shirts or something with a small pattern. Years ago when Regis Philbin had the show *Who Wants to be a Millionaire,* he started a new trend of the monochromatic look, where the tie and the shirts were the same color. That doesn't work in our industry at all. Don't wear yellow shirts, don't wear purple shirts. Be sure to send your shirts to the laundry versus washing them yourself. If you are traveling make sure to touch up your shirts with an iron. It's a conservative business whether you like it or not. And again it goes back to if this isn't your cup of tea, then look for another line of work. Look for another business.

Should it be button-down collar? Should it be spread collars? That goes to the culture of the particular territory. You need to dress for the people that you're going to see. For quite a few years, I covered North and South Dakota, where spread collars and French cuffs weren't appropriate for that part of the world. However having a well-ironed button-down collar shirt and button-cuffed shirt was the expected appropriate dress. If I'm working in large metropolitan areas - New York, Denver, Houston, Los Angeles - I lean more towards French cuffs with cuff links and a spread-collared shirt. But again, keep it basic.

For women, I think it's exactly the same thing. Women have a little bit more leeway with beautiful blouses, but they should always be fresh looking, always ironed and should match the business suit, whether the business suit on Monday includes slacks and on Tuesday a skirt. Business dress should be conservative, clean, crisp and professional looking.

Men have a real advantage with ties because as conservative as shirts and suits maybe, you can always make a great statement by having a great-looking, bright tie. Realize that the old IBM look of a navy blue suit, white shirt and a solid red tie can get a little bit boring. So if you have a dark gray suit, or you're wearing a pinstripe suit and you've got a white shirt on, you can have a great-looking tie underneath it that makes a statement and adds a little color to an otherwise conservative look.

Socks.....you may ask why I would be talking about socks. There seems to be a trend these days of younger folks wearing beautiful suits only to reveal socks with strange stripes, patterns and colors or no socks at all as soon as they sit down. Again, that's fine if you're going out on a date but at work it should be black socks or navy blue socks period. Calf-high socks work well when you sit down. As trivial as it may sound, it doesn't look very professional to be showing skin in the middle of a meeting should your pant legs get pushed up.

Socks of course lead to shoes. Shoes need to be just as conservative as the rest of your business outfit; and that means more often than not black dress shoes. Although there seems to be a trend wearing brown shoes with dark suits, especially navy blue suits; the color black would be the more conservative choice. You can probably line up a lot of people and get just as many opinions for or against brown shoes and dark suits. Moreover, your dress shoes need to be in good condition with decent soles and heels on them and not be run down or unpolished. You should **never** walk in anybody's office with a pair of scuffed-up shoes.

Women need to pay attention to their shoes, too. Often some women will take great pride in everything that they are wearing but never look at the condition of their shoes. Women need to get their shoes shined as much as, if not more than, men. Their shoes need to be looking just as great as the rest of their outfit.

Let me take a moment to touch on jewelry. In my opinion less is more. Wearing too much "bling" can be a distraction. I've seen some men wearing a big watch on the outside of their shirt cuff. What they don't realize, is that it distracts from the purpose of the meeting, which is having the client pay attention to what you are saying. Are you trying to show off or are you trying to sell something? If a client is distracted by a gigantic watch on the cuff of your shirt, that isn't helping the sales process at all. That just sends a message of arrogance.

The moral of this chapter is that you want people to compliment you on the way you look, because you look professional, someone who can be trusted. The whole idea here is that "first impression". When a client first sees you, do you look successful? Wearing shabby, ill fitting or un-pressed clothes or having shoes that aren't shined, gives a potential client the impression that you are not successful. And people don't want to do business with unsuccessful people. A successful person wants to do business with other successful people.

Let's switch gears from personal appearance to something that can be just as important in making an impression on your client, your car. Your car, in essence, is your office and more times than not, you are taking a client to breakfast, lunch or dinner and they want to ride with you. So when they come out and take a look at your car, they're going to form an immediate impression about you. You don't have to drive a Rolls or a Bentley to impress your clients, but you must follow some simple guidelines:

Number one: always drive a four door car. More times than not, you will be driving more than one person to a restaurant. One thing I have noticed with young wholesalers is a car seat for their kids in the backseat. Are you running a business, or are you running a daycare? Now I understand that you may have to pick up your kids from daycare, but the car seat should stay out of your car during business hours. There is nothing worse than your clients trying to sit comfortably around the car seat in your backseat. Again, many may disagree with this attitude but it's an impression. Impressions affect all that you do.

Your car should always be clean, both inside and out. This mean washing and vacuuming your car at least once a week. I've seen many wholesalers who because they are running hard go through the drive-thru at Starbucks or McDonald's, and as a result the backseat is full of hamburger wrappers or empty coffee cups. That should never be the case. Make sure the trash is gone before your next call.

Something else that needs your attention is the trunk of your car. More times than not, following lunch with a client, the client will request an extra piece or two of literature and they're standing there as you open your trunk. What do they see? Your laundry, your golf clubs or literature scattered everywhere? No! Your trunk should be just as clean as the interior of your car and very organized so you easily access the piece of literature they requested.

Again, it's the little things that add up to a client's impression of whom and with whom they're doing business. Are you a successful pro or are you just being haphazard about everything that you do?

One last point on cars; the same rules apply to rentals. You should always rent a mid- or full-size, never a compact car. You never know when you're going to have to transport clients or maybe your boss. It should always be a four door. I don't care if the counter person at Hertz says, "Hey, for no extra money I'm going to give you a Mustang Convertible to drive." You need to get the right car for your business and always anticipate the unexpected; whether it happens or not.

Thread #4: Knowledge

"Today knowledge has power. It controls access to opportunity and advancement."
-Peter F. Drucker

Knowledge can mean a lot of different things: knowledge about your product, knowledge about your competition, knowledge about your client and your client's financial knowledge about what the economy is doing. Most importantly, knowledge is doing your homework. When I was going to school, from elementary through high school and all the way through college, I hated doing homework. I would think of a thousand and one things to do to avoid doing my homework. How I ever graduated is beyond me because I just didn't like doing homework. Now throughout my long career I ironically discovered that homework is often the most valuable tool that I have, and I have learned to take advantage of it. It goes back to running a business like a business, understanding that it is a franchise. I need to know every possible thing that I can about my franchise and everything that goes into it, because knowledge is power.

So, number one. Know your product; know it inside and out. I can't tell you how many wholesalers I know who have never read the literature that they're handing out to their clients about their product. You should always read all the literature.

Although it sounds terribly boring, you'll gain a wealth of knowledge from reading the prospectus. Highlight the key parts and data in the prospectus for a quick reference, when needed. It can expedite finding answers to tough questions. Most of your clients are not going to know nearly as much as you do about your product but there will be certain clients who will ask you very tough questions and it's always good to be prepared. That preparation means reading through the literature and the prospectus. You should be able to show your client how to use the literature with their clients. Like homework, it doesn't sound exciting, but it pays dividends....... you have to do it!

It is one thing to know your product inside and out but the successful wholesalers know where it fits. Earlier we talked about mentors and older colleagues, people who have done it before you. There's no reason to reinvent the wheel. Call some of your senior colleagues. They've been selling products for a long time, and have had much success as well as some failures. Why not have a great conversation with them about those successes and some of the pitfalls. How do they position the product? Again you're not trying to reinvent the wheel, and great sales positioning ideas are invaluable.

You have to remember that people don't go to the store to buy a drill. They go to the store to buy holes.

This is true of anything we sell. You first need to find out what result your product provides. What is its end game? Your senior colleagues have that knowledge. Having them share it with you, will save a lot of homework time.

You also need to know your competitor's products. Not for the sake of beating up on them, but clients really appreciate somebody who is just as knowledgeable about the competition as they are of their own product. It helps them make an educated, knowledgeable decision as to what will work best for their own client. After all no one product fits every need. Probably the highest compliment that a wholesaler can be paid is when he/she is constantly called by their clients with questions. And not just questions about their own product but questions about the industry or about competitors. That's a great indicator that they trust your opinion. When you become that trusted resource because of your knowledge base, you win by default.

Next you need to know your industry. Whether it is the financial services industry, the pharmaceutical industry or any other industry for that matter, they all are constantly changing. Be an expert on what is currently happening in your industry, whether it is sales or government regulation; this again makes you a valuable resource to your clients. Something that is often overlooked at time is knowledge of our client's sentiment toward the industry. These are all things that come into account when you're trying to make a sale.

Know the firms with whom you're dealing. Wirehouses in the case of financial services industry have different ways of doing business than independent brokers dealers. You need to know the firms attitude about wholesalers making calls on their offices and on their advisors. When you first call on that Merrill Lynch branch the last thing you need to do is make the branch manager mad because you unknowingly violated one of his/her rules about calling on the office.

One tool that is rarely used by financial services wholesalers is their firm's relationship team or their national account team. Most firms these days have a team of people who are in charge of maintaining the relationship with specific firms. Those people can be a tremendous wealth of knowledge about who the players are in that firm, what their rules and regulations are; what their prerogatives about doing business are; what their attitudes are about doing business in some areas. So, I would strongly suggest you utilize those folks.

Finally, but it is cardinal rule number one: **Know Thy Client!** You need to know as much about your client as you possibly can. If you're making your very first call on a client, use your CRM systems or database systems, to prepare. These systems generally contain some history of that client, and they can provide you a lot of information before you even walk in the door. You should know whether that client has done business with your firm or not. Did they once do business then quit, why? Are they a senior, top producer at their firm or a guy in the bullpen? You need to know all of these things. In this era of Google, LinkedIn, etc. there should be no excuse not to research the clients you are seeing for the first time.

When you do meet with the client don't be so myopic. A huge mistake I see young wholesalers make is that they are so focused on the client they fail to open their eyes and see what's around them. The client's office is a reflection of the client, therefore a wealth of information for you the wholesaler. If they have nothing but family pictures on their credenza, you know that family is really, really important to them. Do they have golf pictures, sailing pictures, or fishing pictures? By looking around you can discover what is important to that person. That also suggests conversation topics which can create a positive relationship by expressing interest in what interest the client.

My friend Gary Flater, a former financial advisor in the Denver area, once told me "Young wholesalers tend to walk into the advisor's office with the medication without even diagnosing the patient. He's got the solution not even knowing what the problem might be. They get so focused in knowing their product, knowing the competition and all that; they forget to learn about the actual client and what the client needs." You have two eyes, two ears, one mouth. Do more listening and observing than talking.

MIKE NICOLA

Thread #5: Preparation

"One of life's most painful moments comes when we must admit that we didn't do our homework, that we are not prepared"
-Merlin Olsen

When you first get into a territory and then at least on an annual basis, the number one rule of preparation should be to create a one-page business plan. What are your goals, short term and long term? What are you trying to achieve this year? You need to do this every year, because again, it goes back to the fact that this is your franchise. You run your business like a business. You need to have a business plan. Every successful business does. So, why wouldn't you, as a successful franchise owner, regardless of industry, have a business plan?

There are only so many hours in the day, the week, the month, the year, to be productive. How do I work effectively and efficiently in my franchise? It goes back to preparation. Am I prepared for tomorrow and am I prepared for this business year? Many of the things I'm going to suggest are for those of you taking over a territory but they need to be reviewed and refreshed on an annual basis.

First you need to find out how many advisors can sell your product in your territory. I know this sounds obvious and even elementary but I have had wholesalers work for me who couldn't answer that question. How many of them are already selling my product? If you don't know that, then you might as well be throwing darts blindfolded. Once you know how many advisors you have, the first thing to do is segment those advisors into priority groups: A Producers (those producers who account for 80% of the revenue in your territory), B Producers, C Producers and potential prospects. How much time do you want to spend with your "A" Producers versus the rest of the field? Those are questions that you should ask yourself and that should be part of that one-page business plan. It may be just a line in that business plan but it reminds you and keeps you on track. And by the way, your business plan should be carried in your brief case at all times so that you can look at it and remind yourself of the path that you need to travel, the direction that you need to go.

I've known very successful wholesalers who have said, "Instead of only going an inch deep and a mile wide in my territory I'm going an inch wide and a mile deep. I only have time to work with 100 top producing clients in my territory". Finding those people who are your top 100 producers on whom you are going to concentrate on is part of your preparation.

Now that you know on whom to call, what is the most efficient way to cover them?

To start with you need to divide your geographical territory into manageable zones. You make money by being in front of your clients, not in your car or on an airplane. In other words create zones that give you the least amount of time in your car and the maximum amount of time in front of your clients. I've known wholesalers in large metropolitan cities who had a single high-rise as a zone. Whereas, if you are covering multiple states, North Dakota might be a zone. Depending on the size of your territory, you may spend a day in a zone or an entire week.

With your zones created you now create an efficient rotation through those zones. Rotations serve as a map of how to run your territory. It takes the guess work out of where you are going to be in two weeks. Also this doesn't mean that all zones are given equal time. Perhaps you are in Zone One twice as often in your rotation as Zone Two. Again this comes down to what is the most efficient use of your time.

Then this process should be reviewed, managed and adjusted as needed. I'll give you a case in point. When I was wholesaling some years ago, I had seven states to wholesale. It was quite a bit. Each one of these states was a zone in and of itself, and I would manage those individual zones. At the end of the year, I was doing my annual review and business plan for the following year and I found in looking through my production runs that Colorado was doing a lot of business. It was doing a much bigger portion of the business than I was giving it time. So, I adjusted my rotation rather than being in Colorado every seven weeks, I was in Colorado the first week of every single month. Then the rest of the rotation would fall behind it. A year later, I found that Arizona was my second biggest producing zone, so again I adjusted my rotation again. Now I was in Colorado the first week of the month and Arizona the last week of the month. Those middle two weeks, I rotated through North and South Dakota, Nebraska, Utah, etc.

You can constantly adjust your zones and rotation as you do your homework. Look at the numbers. Look at the number of calls you're making. Look at the number of producers, and fine tune it from time to time. Every successful person does this. Great athletes make adjustments all the time to enhance their performance and so should you.

And finally, have your 52 week rotation in writing and in your briefcase all of the time. The simplest way I found to do this is to simply create a one page Word document with all 52 weeks of the year with which zone I'm going to be in each week. Then print it, stick it in a plastic sleeve and put it in your briefcase. The reason I like to do it as a Word document is it is easy to return to the document to make adjustments. Remember your rotations may be adjusted by you and by unforeseen things like a divisional or national sales meeting. The reason you should carry it with you is simple; you can't set the next appointment before you leave the client's office, if you don't know when you'll be back in that zone. This is especially true in Wirehouses. I'm going to state the obvious here, make sure your Internal partner has your 52 week scheduled rotation on his/her desk all of the time.

Speaking of internals, most financial services companies will pair one internal with one external wholesaler. As a Wholesaler I considered my Internal a partner in my franchise and perhaps the most powerful tool I had. Since wholesalers are "fast moving targets," it's hard at times for the advisor to get in touch with them on a timely basis if they have a question or a problem. A good internal who feels like they have ownership in your franchise and who can develop strong relationships with your advisors is invaluable. They become the go to person in your absence. As I mentioned earlier, the internal should have your advisor segmentation as well as your zones and rotation. If you own the franchise then your internal is not only your partner but he/she is your business manager. Leverage their knowledge and resourcefulness and by all means, never take them for granted.

Let's talk for a moment about scheduling appointments. One of the things that I hated to do as a wholesaler was set appointments. It seemed like I was constantly playing telephone tag with the advisor or the advisor's assistant. I would be in my car driving from one appointment to another trying to get appointments scheduled for a week or two weeks out, and it was just maddening. One solution that a lot of wholesalers do is to take an office day once a week. Well as my National Sales Manager, Bob Cassato once told me, "Think about that. If you're taking an office day every week, you're eliminating 20% of your selling time."

I took that to heart, so I decided I would eliminate the one part of the job I hated and give it to someone else to do, and in the process I became more productive. So for virtually my entire wholesaling career, I had an outside scheduler schedule my appointments. Now the person who I happened to hire had some experience being an assistant at a Merrill Lynch office and knew how to speak to financial advisors. She quit Merrill when she started having children and wanted to work from home. I gave her my segmented list of advisors, my zones and rotations and let her set up the appointments. She quickly became a partner with me and my internal. My internal and my scheduler were in constant communication. For instance, the scheduler may try to schedule an appointment with somebody and they would say, "We're busy but we can use a couple more product kits." Well, then the scheduler would call my internal and get that going. The flipside of that is that my internal would be talking to one of my clients and the client would say, "When's the next time Mike is going to be in town? I would really love to see him." Then my internal would call my scheduler and ask her to schedule an appointment with that advisor the next time I was in town. It was a very simple, efficient and successful partnership.

Some people have said advisors don't like to talk to schedulers, or schedulers don't know enough about the product or they're not licensed. My scheduler wasn't selling the product, she was selling the appointment. She knew it was a Variable Annuity or a Mutual Fund but beyond that she had my internal call the advisor to answer any questions. Plus most of the time my scheduler wasn't talking to the advisor but was talking with the advisor's assistant who kept his/her calendar. In my entire career of wholesaling I had a scheduler from beginning to end, I never had even one advisor push back on the fact that my scheduler called to set up the appointment, not one time. So, I'm a big fan of it, but again it's how you want to run your business. One side note on schedulers; most of the time I paid my scheduler out of my pocket as an independent contractor, and as a contract laborer they were responsible for their own taxes and had no benefits. Some companies will allow you to expense a scheduler. I would just check with your company's senior management. (By the way if your manager doesn't think it's worthwhile to have a scheduler, have them call me.)

That's what this book is about. This is another "common" thread that can lead to success but it's still your business and you have to be comfortable in what you do because when you are comfortable, you're more successful.

One last thought on preparation; that is preparing for the week ahead. One of the most successful wholesalers who ever worked for me was a gentleman by the name of Steve Scanlon in Dallas, Texas. You'd think that your company's number one producer would not take the time to do his weekly paper work or bother preparing for the week ahead. Steve was religious about it. I knew where to find Steve at 10:00AM Central Time every Sunday of the year. He was in his office getting ready for his upcoming week. He was in his office doing his expense reports and his activity reports. He was in getting prepared for the people he was going to see that week. He was doing his homework!

One time I asked Steve, "Why is it always Sunday at 10:00?" He said, "That's when football starts. Even when it's outside of football season, it just became such a habit for me to be in my office at 10 on Sunday mornings. Sometimes I'll be there for a half hour and sometimes I'll be there for two or three hours getting ready." This led to one thing, Monday morning when the alarm went off, he was ready to go to work. He didn't have to do any prep work on Monday morning, it was all ready done. All of his administrative chores that he had to do in order to run a good franchise, run a business like a business, were completed on Sunday. Thus the rest of the week was nothing but selling.

Part of his preparation was doing quick reviews of his business plan and asking himself if he was on track. In scuba diving there is an old saying, "Plan your dive, then dive your plan". It's no different than preparing to successfully run your franchise.

Thread #6: Etiquette

*"Good manners will open doors
that the
best education cannot"*
-Clarence Thomas

So far we have talked about the important "common threads" of Attitude, Appearance, Knowledge and Preparation in running a successful franchise. There is another element that I think is just as important: etiquette. We'll touch on a broader sense of etiquette in my next book *Direct Selling* but let's discuss how it goes hand in hand with preparation.

Etiquette is doing little things like knowing the geography of the zone in which you are working; being on time because you know the drive time between appointments. Aside from pure arrogance, to me there is nothing ruder than being late. This is your client and they are busy. They shouldn't have to wait on you. There should be no reason other than something that is unforeseen like an accident or a flat tire, for being late. It's just common courtesy to be on time, it's a sign of respect.

Another part of etiquette is to never disregard the receptionist or the advisor's assistant. You should be treating the receptionist and assistant as well as you treat the advisor. They are the gate-keepers. Not only do these people have control over whom if anyone you will see in the office but they have tremendous behind the scenes influence on which product the advisor shows their clients. So, being courtesy and knowing their names is really important.

The next person to whom you should show a lot of respect, and it is just simple etiquette, is the Branch Manager. If you are calling on an office for the first time, the very first call should not be with advisor, it should be a one-on-one appointment with the manager of the office. To have any success in that office, you need to find out what the manager looks for in wholesalers and how you can help him or her. It's just simple etiquette: this is *their* franchise so find out what their business plan is. How can they incorporate you? How can you help them? If you have the manager as an ally then you pretty much have carte blanche. This goes back to doing your homework. By disrespecting him or her by not having the where with all to set up a preliminary meeting to introduce yourself and finding out how they like their office to be called on, is a huge mistake.

By the way, just because you have some time on your calendar, doesn't mean that you can just drop in on an office. Most managers, regardless of the size of the office, absolutely hate salespeople who just drop in and do quick walk throughs. That is just an absolute no-no. I do know of tenured wholesalers who have been thrown out of major branches and eventually thrown out of firms because they thought they could walk in whenever they wanted and talk to whomever they wanted. Even if I had an appointment with a specific advisor in a branch, I would always make sure the Manager knew it was a set appointment and not an unplanned walk through. The fact is, it's their "house" and as a guest we need to respect them and their rules.

Speaking of respect, a wholesaler should never sit down until they are invited to sit down by the advisor. They should remain standing until the advisor sits down, then sit down, or if the advisor says, "Go ahead and sit down, I'm getting a cup of coffee." But you should never sit down before you're invited to sit down, that includes in the conference room also. If you've been shown into the conference room and the advisor is going to join you there, you should not sit down until the advisor comes in and invites you to sit down. Its little things like that, which shows respect. It's just being polite.

Over the years I've interviewed a lot of people and have had institutional wholesalers call me. If they come in my office and they plop down in the chair before I've invited them to or before I've even gotten around my desk, they're all ready ten points in the hole with me, and it's going to take a while for them to dig out. Most of them don't. So, again, it's little things.

And then lastly, don't overstay your welcome. Don't just keep rambling on about your product hoping the advisor is going to give in. These are busy people, just like you. You should make your point and if it's a 15-minute call, it's a 15-minute call. If they want to keep engaging you and keep you there for 45 minutes, let them do the engaging. But make your case, ask for the order and then get out.

MIKE NICOLA

Thread #7: Personal Care

"Energy and persistence conquer all things"
-Benjamin Franklin

We've talked throughout this whole book about being a franchise of one, Mr. Wholesaler, Inc., and just like any franchise you need to keep that franchise in good shape. So, why don't we talk about what you have to do in order to run a franchise of one?

In a franchise of one that creates $100 million in production, it takes a lot of energy. And by energy, you have to be in good shape to run hard … you are a one-person show. Yes, you may have a teammate like your internal, but your internal isn't getting in and out of the car six, seven or eight times a day or dragging literature around.

I'll refer to a great story that actually happened a few years ago. An internal was complaining about what a cushy job their external wholesaler had and the wholesaler heard about it. The next time she was in the home office, the wholesaler along with the national sales manager approached this internal and said, "Here's what we want you to do today. We're on the eighth floor, and at a quarter to every hour, we want you to go down and out to your car, get into your car, close the door, start the car, turn the car off, get out of your car, and come back up to your desk. And we want you to do that every hour throughout the day, including your lunch hour." By the end of the day that internal was exhausted and never complained again about her external partner.

Now that doesn't sound like much, riding the elevator up and down, getting in and out of your car with literature as you make your daily calls; but when you couple that with the energy you need to make a good presentation you need to be in shape physically and emotionally. So, there are some things that you need to do for yourself in order to be that franchise of one.

Number one, do you get enough sleep? You can't be the last person at the bar every night if you're entertaining clients. You need to get in and get some sleep. You need to eat right and watch what you eat. The consequence of this job is that you end up eating a lot of meals in restaurants, in hotels or on airplanes. You need to watch what you eat.

This is a very social business and drinking with advisors can be part of it, to the point of where it can be obsessive. Keep in mind that if you drink too much, your professionalism goes out the door. Also, alcohol is a dehydrator and it can severely dehydrate your body. If you wake up in the morning and you're dehydrated or you're hung over, you're not at the top of your game. You need to watch that.

It helps if you can work out daily or at least three or four times a week. Now, if you're a busy wholesaler and you're starting with a 7:00AM breakfast meeting, not getting home until 4 or 5 in the afternoon and then you're taking care of your family, it's hard to find time to get a workout in. There are a lot of great 30-minute workouts. It just takes 30-minutes three, four or five times a week to keep you in shape.

Anytime you bring travel in to play, where you're sleeping in different beds, eating in restaurants and driving different cars, it puts stress on your body. There're a lot of little nuances that go with traveling and working your plan that you need to have down. A lot of people say, "Well, wholesaling is a glamorous job. You're a "preferred frequent flyer" so you probably get upgraded; you eat out at nice restaurants; you drink good wine." Anyone who has done this job knows that it gets old, and it can be hard on you, if you're not in good physical shape.

Psychologically you need to have a life away from work also. Too many of us are obsessed with success. We're obsessed with doing a great job, pleasing our boss, pleasing the company and making money, that we forget to have a life. Walk away from the job from time to time just for your own mental health. My wife will laugh at this because I'm the biggest offender but in your career you should not forget about your family. You want to be successful so you can provide a good life for your family but in doing so it's easy to forget about them or unconsciously ignore them. They're your biggest support system. So, don't forget about your support system. It will keep you in good mental and emotional shape.

Years ago when I was wholesaling and covering seven states I was leaving every Monday morning and coming home Friday afternoons or evenings. My kids were young, my daughter was three-years-old. I came home one Friday evening, with my suit on, my tie was kind of pulled down and my shirt was unbuttoned at the collar. I'm saying hello to everybody and my wife says, "How about if we go out tonight? I've got a babysitter, how about dinner or a movie?" And I start to grimace. I've been eating in restaurants all week. I just got off a two-hour flight. I'm tired. My wife catches me rolling my eyes at the idea of going out. At that point she walked over, grabbed the lapels of my suit coat, got nose to nose with me and said, "You don't understand, but the most intelligent conversation I've had this past week is with a three-year-old." At that moment I realized my support team at home was working just as hard as I was and I needed to take care of them.

Successful wholesalers take care of themselves physically, mentally and emotionally. That's why I would strongly suggest that taking care of you should be a part of your business plan, too. Try to get that 30-minute workout in. Try to take the stress off. Try to spend some quality time with your family. All of this goes right back to Thread #2: Attitude. People see it in your face; the clients with whom you are meeting see it. If you're feeling good, your attitude is much better. If you don't have a lot of stress at home, more than normal I should say, your attitude is better. There are a lot of different things that go along with that.

Conclusion

In conclusion I would urge all of you to do one thing before you walk out the door and open your mouth. Check "your threads". Ask yourself these questions:

How's my attitude today?

Do I look like a professional? Or do I look like an unmade bed?

Am I confident in my knowledge? Am I prepared for the day? There are always going to be unexpected things that are thrown at me but am I as prepared as I can possibly be?

Has my etiquette become second nature to me or am I still fumbling with it?

Have I been taking care of myself?

One of my most influential mentors, Doug Wood, always told all of us who worked for him and I'm quoting him, "Right before you leave for the day, look in a full-length mirror and ask yourself, 'Would I do business with that person?' If the honest answer is not a resounding 'Yes', you would be better off going back to bed."

Best of luck! Here's to weaving these Threads into a successful career and life!

MIKE NICOLA

www.ingramcontent.com/pod-product-compliance
Lightning Source LLC
Chambersburg PA
CBHW021930170526
45157CB00005B/2262